D1731854

© Copyright Dadda Panda Books 2023 - All rights reserved.

The content contained within this book may not be reproduced, duplicated or transmitted without direct written permission from the author or the publisher. Under no circumstances will any blame or legal responsibility be held against the publisher, or author, for any damages, reparation, or monetary loss due to the information contained within this book. Either directly or indirectly. You are responsible for your own choices, actions, and results.

Legal Notice:
This book is copyright protected. This book is only for personal use. You cannot amend, distribute, sell, use, quote or paraphrase any part, or the content within this book, without the consent of the author or publisher.

Disclaimer Notice:
Please note the information contained within this document is for educational and entertainment purposes only. All effort has been executed to present accurate, up to date, and reliable, complete information. No warranties of any kind are declared or implied. Readers acknowledge that the author is not engaging in the rendering of legal, financial, medical or professional advice. The content within this book has been derived from various sources. Please consult a licensed professional before attempting any techniques outlined in this book. By reading this document, the reader agrees that under no circumstances is the author responsible for any losses, direct or indirect, which are incurred as a result of the use of the information contained within this document, including, but not limited to, — errors, omissions, or inaccuracies.

OUR GIFT TO YOU

As a special thanks for getting this book, we'd like to offer you a special gift. Dadda Panda has worked with his friend, Sarah Bushell RD to produce:

10 STRATEGIES TO ENCOURAGE PICKY EATERS TO TRY NEW FOODS.

To get your copy
simply visit
www.daddapanda.com
or scan the QR code

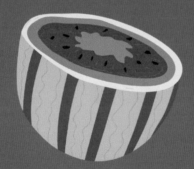

Panda twins Bamboo and Blossom
think their dad is really awesome.

He's a brilliant dad that is always there.
A kind hearted and loving,
big panda bear.

Who loves to tell funny jokes,
so very cheeky.

And is a master at hide and seek,
very very sneaky.

He lets the twins dress him up in fun
and silly clothes.

And together they take selfies
and strike a funny pose.

And even in strange places,
Dadda Panda loves to sing.

And when they go to the playground,
he's the first to take the swing.

And when the twins feel sad
he'll give them a big squeeze,
because a Dadda Panda
hug puts everyone at ease.

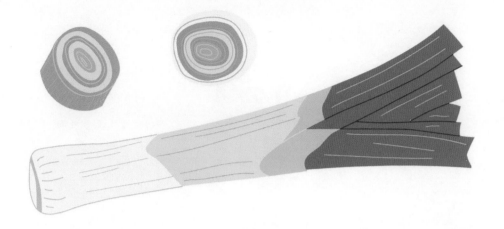

But where Dadda Panda isn't yet
a winner, is when it comes
to making dinner.
Because little Blossom and
bouncing Bamboo,
never like to eat something new.

For them nuggets and pasta
are the rage.

But these foods are terribly beige.

"Cabbage, broccoli,
that's disgusting!
Peas and cauliflower
those belong in the dustbin."

The kids were simply stuck
in their ways.
Eating the same food
on most of the days.

"You might really like them!"
Dadda Panda cries,
"Nobody knows until somebody tries!"

"Don't dismiss it or just assume,
I bet you'll both like a tasty mushroom."

"Mushroom, Yuk,"
said the cheeky two.
"We won't even give it a chew!"

So Dadda Panda has made a decision.
It's time to make this his mission.

A time to be bold, a time to be brave,
he makes his way to the "The Dad Cave."

After tapping a special button on his chest, the cave transforms into a gadget filled nest.

More than just an ordinary shed,
it's a place where Dadda Panda
can really think ahead.

And in the corner what can you spy?
A very smart-plant called Bot-Zai.

It looks like a tree but believe it or not,
it's actually a very useful magic robot.

Dadda Panda calls -
"Bot-Zai! Bot-Zai!
I need a favour,
The kids won't try a new flavour!
Mushroom or broccoli they're not a fan
Please help me however you can."

Bot-Zai responds:
"Just hide the good food,
and don't tell a soul.
They won't know what they're
eating it, that's the goal.
Mash it, blend it, put the new
food in disguise.

It's their favorite dish with added lies."

'That's not the way'
Dadda Panda cried.
"Surely the answer is not to hide?"

"I want the kids to actually like a
new food, and telling them
fibs feels rather rude!"

Bot-Zai replies "Ok, then give them food they don't like!
And tell them they have to eat it or you'll go on strike!"

That doesn't feel right!"
Dadda Panda states.
"I want the kids to actually like
their plates."

Bot-Zai huffs "I've given you ideas and you don't like one! Trying to help you isn't much fun."

Fun! That's it!"
Dadda Panda has started to see,
"New food should be joyful
and full of glee.
Trying new food is tasty and
so much fresher
I need to make it fun
without the pressure."

"Erm…I knew I could help" Bot-Zai
said with a puzzled tone
"But now it's time for you to
LEAF me alone."

"Very good"
Dadda replies with a smile
"It's time to complete the mission,
Dadda Panda style."

Dadda Panda starts by creating the most wonderful scene.
A veggie trail that's all fresh and green.

Bamboo and Blossom follow along,
while Dadda Panda sings the
"**GOBBLE YOUR GREENS**" song.

And guess where the trail lead?
To the most incredible food spread.
With different ingredients that
make up faces.
Different foods that look like places.

And to Dadda Panda's surprise,
Blossom wasn't shy.
And held up a green bean
to give it a try.

She gave it a bite, all rather hasty,
and thought 'Wow that's really tasty.'
"This is delicious" she said with glee.
But her brother Bamboo didn't agree.

"I don't want to try beans,
broccoli or peas!
But I will have some of that scrummy
pasta please?"

Dadda Panda grinned
"I'm glad the pasta is a hit,
Now let's try mixing it up a bit."
"Pasta is perfect for adding
something new."
Make it fun or silly, it's up to you!"

So Blossom added mushroom,
peppers and corn,
And abracadabra a new dish was born!

But Bamboo didn't think
much of the trick
"I think this mixed up dish
will make me sick."
So while Blossom was busy tucking in,
stubborn Bamboo refused to begin.

But Dadda knew
he could win,
he just had to believe.

And luckily he had one last trick up his sleeve...

Because in the garden
without the kids knowing.
A beautiful broccoli plant
was secretly growing.
With beautiful leaves
and a mini-tree on top
This didn't look like food from the shop.
Dadda Panda showed the kids
his special surprise
And they really couldn't believe
their eyes.

Dadda Panda said
"give it some water and plenty of light
And before you know it
you can take a bite"
Bamboo cheered
"my very own Broccoli plant,
how amazing."
And he watched it slowly grow,
while constantly gazing.

Soon it was time to pick the mini-tree,
cook it up and have it for tea.

Bamboo gave it a try
without hesitation,
which was a cause for a big
celebration.

"This is delicious,"
shouted a happy Bamboo.
"I really like trying something new."

And with that there was no going back.
The kids were even eating veggies
as a snack!

It was amazing to see all the
new foods the kids would eat
And so Dadda Panda's Fussy Eating
mission was now complete.

NOW IT'S TIME TO GET CREATIVE!

Colour in these delicious looking veggies
and why not add some of your own.

THESE PLATES NEED SOME FOOD!

Draw your favourite ingredients,
remember to mix it up and have fun!

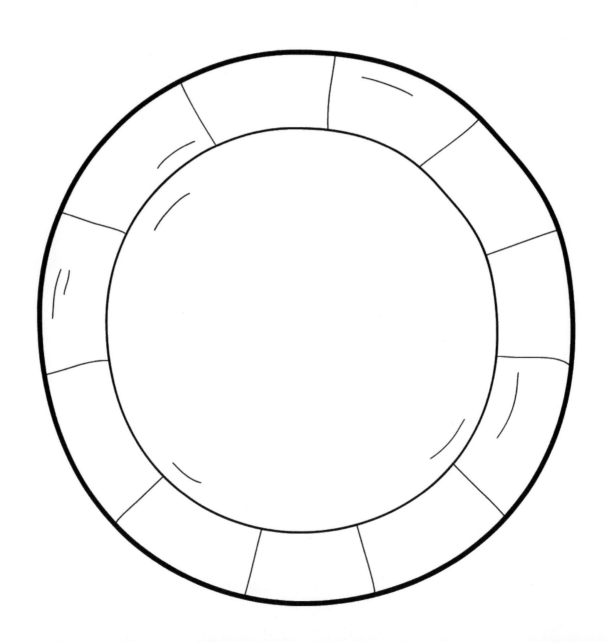

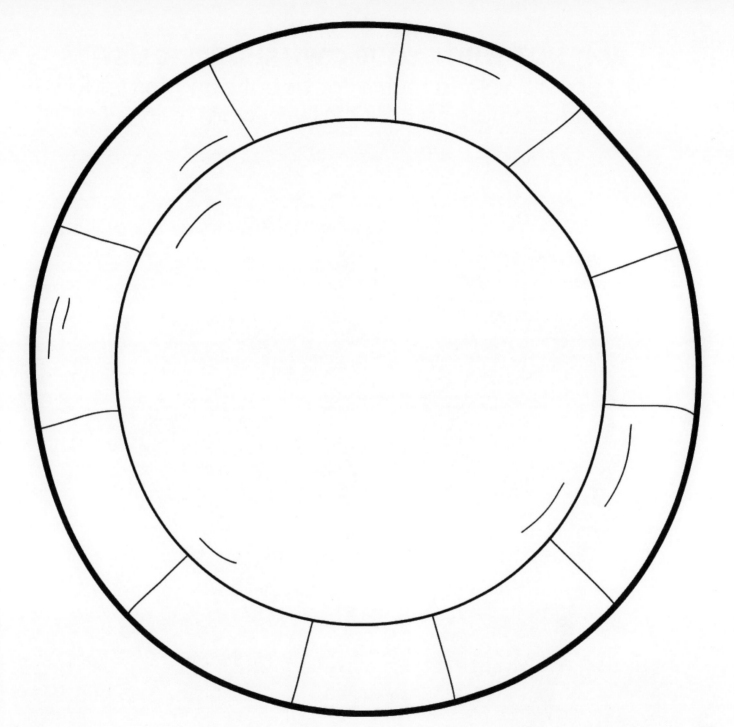

WHY NOT WRITE YOUR OWN SHOPPING LIST!

Fill it up with your favourite foods but don't forget to add something new that you want to try.

SHOPPING LIST

"A new food I've not tried before

SHOPPING LIST

_____

_____

_____

_____

_____

_____

_____

"A new food
I've not
tried before

_____

_____

_____

"USEFUL EXPERTS"

Your fussy eating journey doesn't have to end here.
Here are some brilliant experts who we would highly recommend
you exploring if you need more fussy eating help.

CIARA ATWELL

Ciara Attwell is a mum to two children and founder of the website
My Fussy Eater where she shares healthy eating recipes to feed the whole
family, along with tips and tricks for dealing with picky eaters.
Ciara started sharing her recipes and tips online in 2014 in an attempt to
get her daughter eating a better and more varied diet.
She continues to share these on her website and social media accounts,
along with her recipe App and three cookbooks.

https://www.myfussyeater.com/

BASED
IN
UK

EMMA SHAFQAT, BA, BSC[HONS], RD

I'm Emma Shafqat, a registered paediatric dietitian with over 8 years of
experience. Having worked in the NHS, schools, and privately, I specialise in
supporting families through the challenges of their child's dietary concerns.
As a mum who has conquered fussy eating with my own daughter,
I bring not only professional expertise but also practical, real-world solutions to
transform mealtimes for your family.

https://dietitianwithadifference.co.uk/

BASED
IN
UK

RACHEL ROTHMAN, MS, RD, CLEC

Rachel is a pediatric dietitian and feeding expert and the founder of Nutrition In Bloom, which offers practical, evidence-based support to children with feeding difficulties and their families.

Rachel has helped thousands of families create happier stress-free meals, and specializes in working with neurodiverse children and those with sensory challenges, feeding difficulties and other disorders. Her goal is to help children develop healthy and positive relationships with food – that last a lifetime.

https://nutritioninbloom.com/

BASED
IN
USA

DANIELLE BINNS, BA, CNP

Danielle Binns is a Certified Nutritionist and Picky Eating Expert.
As a mother of three, Danielle understands the feeding struggle intimately, having navigated the challenges of a daughter labeled 'failure to thrive' and an extremely picky eater. Through relentless research and feeding certifications, Danielle turned her own mealtime stress into success, with a daughter who is now one of the most adventurous eaters.

Danielle has since developed a proven formula for adventurous eating and become a beacon of hope for families. Over the past decade, she has helped thousands of children and parents worldwide through her online programs (e.g. "Picky Eater Protocol") as well as her private coaching. If you're ready to reclaim joy at the table and raise a healthy, confident eater, Danielle Binns is your go-to ally.

https://www.daniellebinns.com/

BASED
IN
CANADA

SPECIAL THANKS

A huge thanks to a wonderful team for bringing this book together.
It simply would not have been possible without you.

To Kingbee - to Martyn, Raquel, Gwen and Alex for their wonderful
work, and especially to Kate for all her extra love and dedication in
bringing this book and the songs to life.

To the DaddiLife team - to Jon for his brilliant builds, and especially to
Nick for crafting the wonderful words of Dadda Panda.

A huge thank you too to Sarah Bushell for fantastic insight in helping
us blend real life tips into this children's story.

Printed by Amazon Italia Logistica S.r.l.
Torrazza Piemonte (TO), Italy

54637205R00038